P9-DMV-150

MEXICO

Leading the Southern Hemisphere

Beautiful Diversity
The Geography of Mexico

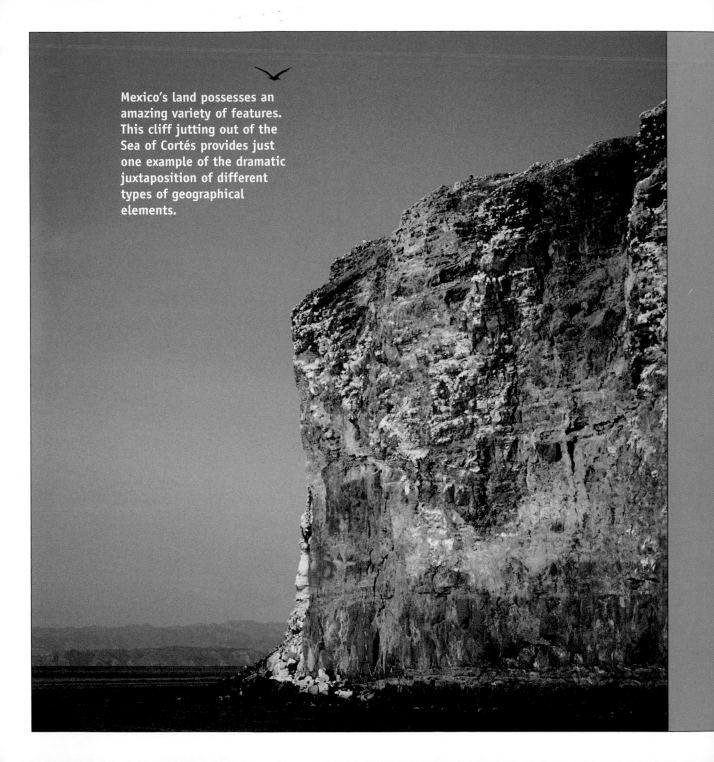

Mexico's land possesses an amazing variety of features. This cliff jutting out of the Sea of Cortés provides just one example of the dramatic juxtaposition of different types of geographical elements.

MEXICO
Leading the Southern Hemisphere

BEAUTIFUL DIVERSITY
THE GEOGRAPHY OF MEXICO

MASON CREST
PHILADELPHIA

Mason Crest
450 Parkway Drive, Suite D
Broomall, PA 19008
www.masoncrest.com

Printed and bound in the United States of America.

CPSIA Compliance Information: Batch #M2014.
For further information, contact Mason Crest at 1-866-MCP-Book.

First printing
1 3 5 7 9 8 6 4 2

Library of Congress Cataloging-in-Publication Data
        on file at the Library of Congress

        ISBN: 978-1-4222-3214-9 (hc)
        ISBN: 978-1-4222-8679-1 (ebook)

Mexico: Leading the Southern Hemisphere series ISBN: 978-1-4222-3213-2

TABLE OF CONTENTS

MEXICO
Leading the Southern Hemisphere

KEY ICONS TO LOOK FOR:

 Text-dependent questions: These questions send the reader back to the text for more careful attention to the evidence presented there.

 Words to understand: These words with their easy-to-understand definitions will increase the reader's understanding of the text, while building vocabulary skills.

 Series glossary of key terms: This back-of-the book glossary contains terminology used throughout this series. Words found here increase the reader's ability to read and comprehend higher-level books and articles in this field.

 Research projects: Readers are pointed toward areas of further inquiry connected to each chapter. Suggestions are provided for projects that encourage deeper research and analysis.

 Sidebars: This boxed material within the main text allows readers to build knowledge, gain insights, explore possibilities, and broaden their perspectives by weaving together additional information to provide realistic and holistic perspectives.

TIMELINE

10,000 B.C.	Valley of Mexico becomes home to first inhabitants.
1200–400 B.C.	Rise and fall of Olmec Civilization; the Maya begin their rise.
A.D. 300–900	Mayan culture is at its peak.
900–1000	Toltecs settle in Valley of Mexico.
1325	Aztecs found the city of Tenochtitlán.
1517–1521	Spanish invasion and conquest of Mexico.
1521–1821	Spanish Colonial era of Mexico.
1910–1921	Mexican Revolution.
1929	The first formal Mexican political party is born; it is now the Party Revolutionary Institutional, or the PRI.
1985	Earthquake hits Mexico City, killing thousands of people.
1997	Hurricane Pauline strikes the Pacific coastal states of Guerrero and Oaxaca; tsunamis caused by Hurricane Guillermo flood the Cabos San Lucas area of Mexico.
2003	A 7.6-magnitude earthquake kills 29 people and leaves thousands homeless along the central Mexican Pacific coast.
2006	Felipe Calderón elected president.
2007	Archaeologists discover an underground chamber that they believe contains the remains of the Aztec emperor Ahuizotl. Category 5 Hurricane Dean strikes the Yucatán Peninsula, forcing over 30,000 people to evacuate; widespread floods temporarily submerge up to 80 percent of the state of Tabasco and kill several people in landslides.
2008	The Mexican government pledges $42 million to improve sanitation and curb pollution in Acapulco, a Pacific coastal city popular with tourists.

View of the Ik-Kil cenote near Chichen Itza. Cenotes are natural pits or sinkholes that occur when limestone bedrock collapses, exposing groundwater underneath. These unusual geographic formations are found throughout the Yucatán Peninsula, and were sometimes used by the original inhabitants of Mexico for religious ceremonies.

2010 Hurricane Karl strikes the state of Veracruz with deadly force, killing 22 people and causing more than $5.6 billion in property damage.

2012 In March, a powerful earthquake near the border between the states of Guerrero and Oaxaca damages or destroys more than 30,000 homes. In December, Enrique Peña Nieto is sworn in as president of Mexico.

2013 In September, Hurricane Manuel and Hurricane Ingrid cause major flooding in southern Mexico, resulting in extensive property damage and more than 160 deaths.

2014 Joaquin "El Chapo" Guzman, leader of the powerful Sinaloa drug cartel, is arrested by the Mexican military, with the assistance of U.S. authorities.

WORDS TO UNDERSTAND

ecosystems—a natural community that functions as a unit.

tropical—characteristic of a region or climate that is always frost-free, with temperatures warm enough and enough moisture to support year-round plant life.

The different areas of Mexico are home to a range of weather patterns, from hot and arid to cool and rainy. Mexicans must dress accordingly for the weather conditions, wearing clothing and hats that shield them from the elements where appropriate.

HORN OF PLENTY:
THE UNITED MEXICAN STATES

Mexico is a horn of plenty filled with deserts, mountains, *tropical* rain forests, beaches, and plateaus. It is home to the deep sea fishing resorts of Cabo San Lucas, the mountain and jungle bike tours of Troncones, and the desert lava fields of Pinacate. The nation also offers a multitude of ethnic festivals, pre-Columbian ancient ruins, and historic art murals. No wonder this Spanish-speaking country is such a favorite vacation destination for so many Americans. It is truly a land filled with many vastly different sights, sounds, smells, textures, and flavors.

When Americans hear the phrase "south of the border," they think of Mexico, because Mexico is the nation that lies south of the United States' border. Belize and Guatemala border Mexico to the southeast. The Gulf of Mexico and the Caribbean Sea wash along Mexico's eastern shores. The Pacific Ocean and the Gulf of California border the western Mexican coastline.

The Texas-Mexico border follows the winding path of the Río Grande. However, Mexico is almost three times the size of Texas. It is the third-largest country in Latin America. Of the Latin American nations, only Brazil and

11

Argentina cover a larger area.

Mexico is made up of 32 political regions; 31 of these political regions are states, and the other region is home to the nation's capital, Mexico City. This zone is known as the Federal District.

Mexico City is the capital of Mexico. It is also Mexico's largest city. The crown jewel of the United Mexican States covers an area of 571 square miles (1,479 square kilometers). The population of Mexico City, as of the year 2014,

FAST FACTS

Capital City:	Mexico City
Government:	Democratic Republic
Official Currency:	Mexican Peso
Area:	760,300 square miles (1,964,375 square kilometers)
Population:	120,286,655 (2014)
Ethnic groups:	*mestizo* (Native American-Spanish) 60%, Native American 30%, white 9%, others 1%
Religions:	Roman Catholic 82.7%, Pentecostal 1.6%, Jehovah's Witnesses 1.4%, other Evangelical Churches 5%, other 1.9%, none 4.7%, unspecified 2.7% (2010 est.)
Languages:	Spanish, Mayan, Nahuatl, and other regional dialects
Continent:	North America
Climate:	tropical to desert
Terrain:	Coastal lowlands, central high plateaus, deserts, and mountains.
Lowest point:	Laguna Salada, 33 feet (10 meters) below sea level
Highest point:	Citlaltépetl, 18,696 feet (5,665 meters)
Natural resources:	petroleum, silver, copper, gold, lead, zinc, natural gas, timber.

The ancient people of Mexico glorified nature and their gods through the temples they built. The Pyramid of the Sun, as well as many smaller pyramids, stands in the pre-Columbian city of Teotihuacán.

was over 20 million. This makes it one of the largest cities in the world.

Mexico City is also, perhaps, one of the most majestic cities in the world. Mountains surround the city, and great volcanoes stand at its sides. The Pyramid of the Sun and the Pyramid of the Moon are visible in the nearby distance. What's more, it is the oldest and the highest city on the North American continent. Over 600 years old, it sits, as if atop a throne, at an elevation of 7,349 feet (2,267 meters). The ruins of an Aztec temple still stand in the center of the city. This busy metropolis is a city with a long, proud history.

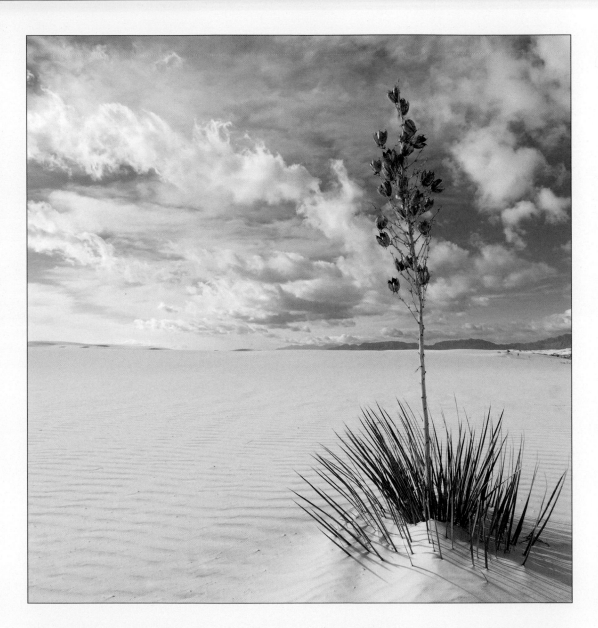

A yucca plant grows in the white, wind-blown sand of the Chihuahuan Desert. Though the land is dry and the air hot in this region, some plants are able to thrive.

Its history begins with the Aztecs who built the ancient foundations of Mexico City on an island in Lake Texcoco over 2,000 years ago. This now crowded modern industrial center was once the center of the Aztec empire. At that time, Mexico City was called Tenochtitlán.

Located in the Valley of Mexico, Mexico City has historically been the center of the nation's population and industrial growth. Nearly one-fifth of the national population lives in or around the capital city. Almost every main north-south transportation route runs through the city.

The other 31 political regions of Mexico are home to a great variety of human, plant, and animal life. Differing elevations and climates have created a wide range of **ecosystems**. Even the soil can change dramatically from place to place within Mexico.

Mexico is, indeed, a horn of plenty filled with many different geographical and historical splendors. Deserts cover

	STATE	CAPITAL
1.	Aguascalientes	Aguascalientes
2.	Baja California	Mexicali
3.	Baja California Sur	La Paz
4.	Campeche	Campeche
5.	Coahuila	Saltillo
6.	Colima	Colima
7.	Chiapas	Tuxtla Gutiérrez
8.	Chihuahua	Chihuahua
9.	Federal District	
10.	Durango	Durango
11.	Guanajuato	Guanajuato
12.	Guerrero	Chilpancingo
13.	Hidalgo	Pachuca
14.	Jalisco	Guadalajara
15.	México	Toluca
16.	Michoacán	Morelia
17.	Morelos	Cuernavaca
18.	Nayarit	Tepic
19.	Nuevo León	Monterrey
20.	Oaxaca	Oaxaca
21.	Puebla	Puebla
22.	Querétaro	Querétaro
23.	Quintana Roo	Chetumal
24.	San Luis Potosí	San Luis Potosí
25.	Sinaloa	Culiacán
26.	Sonora	Hermosillo
27.	Tabasco	Villahermosa
28.	Tamaulipas	Ciudad Victoria
29.	Tlaxcala	Tlaxcala
30.	Veracruz	Xalapa
31.	Yucatán	Mérida
32.	Zacatecas	Zacatecas

16

Mexico's beautiful white sand beaches draw thousands of tourists each year, providing an economic boost. Mexico has become an increasingly popular vacation spot for foreigners, especially Americans.

Cañón del Sumidero in Chiapas began to be formed around the same time as the Grand Canyon in the United States. The Grijalva River runs through the canyon, which has walls as high as 3,280 feet (1,000 meters). The area around Cañón del Sumidero is a Mexican national park.

parts of the nation, while tropical rainforests flourish over others. Volcanoes tower in some areas, while elsewhere lowlands sink slowly toward the seas. Aztec ruins, once the sites of human sacrifices and other mysterious rituals, stand quietly alongside great Catholic cathedrals.

Mexico is a land of great diversity—but the Mexican people are united. Their government, their history, and their love for this great nation draw them together.

TEXT-DEPENDENT QUESTIONS

What river forms the border between Mexico and the U.S. state of Texas?

How many states are there in Mexico?

RESEARCH PROJECT

Most of Mexico, including the central region, is part of the Pacific Ring of Fire, an area where earthquakes and volcanic eruptions occur regularly. Using the Internet or your school library, find out more about the causes of volcanic activity in Mexico and write a one-page report.

WORDS TO UNDERSTAND

Alpine pastures—the mountain slopes above the timberline where low plants grow.

altitude—height.

basin—a hollow in the surface of the land.

plateau—a high, flat land.

salsa—a spicy sauce made from tomatoes, onions, peppers and other ingredients.

temperate—mild or moderate temperatures; neither too hot nor too cold.

tsunamis—tidal waves.

Tall saguaro cacti are silhouetted against the sunset in the Sonoran Desert. This large desert stretches across Mexico and into the United States as well.

HOT, MEDIUM, OR MILD:
THE MANY CLIMATES OF MEXICO

The Tropic of Cancer divides Mexico. It crosses central Mexico and passes through the southern end of Baja California. The part of Mexico that is south of the Tropic of Cancer lies within the earth's tropical climate zone. The part of Mexico that is north of the Tropic of Cancer lies within the earth's **temperate** climate zone.

These two main climate zones, extreme **altitude** changes, and different landscapes work together to create five basic climate areas. Like her spicy **salsas**, Mexico's climate comes in a variety of flavors. At any given moment, somewhere in Mexico, the weather may be red hot, hot, medium, or mild.

The hot land, or *Tierra Caliente,* is the tropical area that falls between sea level and 3,000 feet. The average daily temperature for a tropical city in this area is about 77° Fahrenheit (25° Celsius). This area is an enormous **basin** that begins in the state of Jalisco and continues to the state of Guerrero.

Although Mexico's rainy season starts in May, the Mexican hurricane season doesn't really step into high gear until June.

19

The year 2013 saw an unusually large number of hurricanes developing over the Pacific Ocean. One of them, Hurricane Manuel, originated to the south of Acapulco, and made landfall near Manzanillo on September 14. The storm lasted for seven days, finally breaking apart on September 20.

Satellite view of Hurricane Manual pounding the Pacific Coast of Mexico in September 2013.

At around the same time, another major storm, Hurricane Ingrid, had formed over the Atlantic Ocean. It made landfall on the east coast of Mexico, near La Pesca, Tamaulipas, on September 12, and continued for six days.

Between them, the two storms caused severe flooding in southern Mexico, damaging farmland and housing. More than 160 people were killed—many of them in the Acapulco region—and over 11,500 homes were destroyed by flooding and high winds.

In the aftermath of the storm, the Mexican Army was sent to several places to prevent looting, restore order, and help with relief operations. The government later estimated that more than 1 million Mexicans had been affected by the storms, and that they had caused more than $4.2 billion in damage.

One very special part of tropical Mexico is the Lacandona Rain Forest. This lush tropical rain forest is in the eastern area of Chiapas. Over 4,000 kinds of plants grow in this area. Lacandona's wildlife includes the jaguar, harpy eagles, toucans, scarlet and green macaws, and spider and howler monkeys.

The western half of Lacandona is made up of mountain ranges and narrow valleys. The eastern half of the region is low plains, with secluded hills and valleys. The climate is warm and humid. The average annual temperature is above 75° Fahrenheit (about 24° Celsius).

Mexico's central **plateau** and parts of her highlands are at altitudes between 3,000 and 6,000 feet (about 1,000 to 2,000 meters) above sea level. These areas fall into a climate zone called the *Tierra Templada,* or temperate lands. The average temperatures of this region fall between 60° to 72° Fahrenheit (about 15° to 22° Celsius).

Tierra Fría means the cold land. This climate zone climbs from 6,000

A small stream rushes through the lush rain forest of Chiapas.

21

22

The Nevado de Toluca volcano rises almost 15,000 feet into the sky. The volcano is no longer active; today it is surrounded by forest.

feet to as high as 11,000 feet (about 2,000 to almost 3,000 meters). *Alpine pastures* cover the tops of these altitudes.

Tierra Helada is the Spanish way of saying "the frozen land." This is the name given to the permanent snow line. The frozen land of central Mexico is found at altitudes of 13,000 to 14,000 feet (about 4,000 meters).

Mexico's desert climate is its driest and hottest climate. Most of the largest desert in North America lies south of the border. The Chihuahuan Desert covers more than 200,000 square miles, stretching from just south of Albuquerque, New Mexico, to the state of Zacatecas in Mexico.

In the Chihuahuan Desert, winters are short. For brief periods, however, the temperatures may fall below freezing. Summer temperatures are blistering. The high temperatures are often over 100° (about 38° Celsius). Most of the area receives less than 10 inches of rainfall yearly.

Another North American desert, the Sonoran Desert, covers approximately 120,000 square miles. It covers much of southwestern Arizona and southeastern California. It also extends into most of Baja California and the western half of the state of Sonora, Mexico.

The Sonoran Desert has temperatures of 50° to 60° Fahrenheit (10° to 15° Celsius) even in the winter. In the summer, its temperatures can soar to well above 100° Fahrenheit. Fewer than

Guadalajara's climate is typical of the south-central highlands. This Tierra Templada city has a spring-like climate year round.
Guadalajara is Mexico's second largest city.
A city of festivals, mariachi bands, and artisans, Guadalajara's lovely weather contributes to its happy atmosphere. Its high temperatures average around 80° Fahrenheit (about 27° Celsius), while its lows average around 53°F (about 12°C). With weather like that, no wonder the street bands are always playing!

23

24

Mexico City's climate is a product of both the city's latitude, which is south of the Tropic of Cancer, and its elevation of 7,347 feet (about 2,226 meters). The city is located in a tropical climatic zone. However, its extremely high altitude contributes to its moderate climate. The average annual temperature is about 61° Fahrenheit (16° Celsius). The coldest month of the year is January, when the average ranges from as low as 44° to 70°F (about 7° to 21° C). The warmest month is generally May, when the temperatures range from 54° to 78° F (12° to 25° C).

10 inches of rainfall fall here yearly.

Although little rain falls in Mexico's desert areas, the Mexican rains divide the rest of the country's year into two main seasons. Summer is Mexico's rainy season, lasting from May to October. During this time, there are daily showers throughout most of the country. October to May marks the winter season for most Mexicans, and during the winter, most of the country is subjected to the dry season. Water becomes a precious commodity for many Mexican farmers during these months. Only the northwestern part of Baja California gets most of its rainfall during the winter.

Summer and fall are hurricane season in the coastal areas of Mexico. Mexico's Baja California peninsula becomes increasingly vulnerable to hurricanes beginning in July. Cabo San Lucas and La Paz are also most likely to be hit by

Hurricanes cause significant damage in Mexico each year, as this photo of a resort in Cancún after such a storm shows. These powerful storms typically feature heavy rain and winds blowing at more than 74 miles (119 kilometers) per hour.

hurricanes during July. The biggest hurricane danger for the eastern Mexican coast begins in August and lasts through October. The odds of a hurricane striking Mexico's west coast are at their highest in September.

Several hurricanes per year whirl along the Caribbean and Gulf of Mexico coastline. These storms bring high winds, heavy rain, widespread damage, and sometimes loss of life. In October 1997, for example, Hurricane Pauline caused about 300 deaths when it struck the Pacific coastal states of Guerrero and Oaxaca with terribly destructive force. The most powerful hurricane to hit Mexico from the Atlantic was Hurricane Wilma in 2005, which caused nearly $8 billion in damage and killed 8 people in Mexico.

Hurricanes along the Gulf and the Caribbean coasts are not the only natural disasters that plague Mexico. The country experiences *tsunamis* along the Pacific coast and destructive earthquakes in the center and south. Volcanic

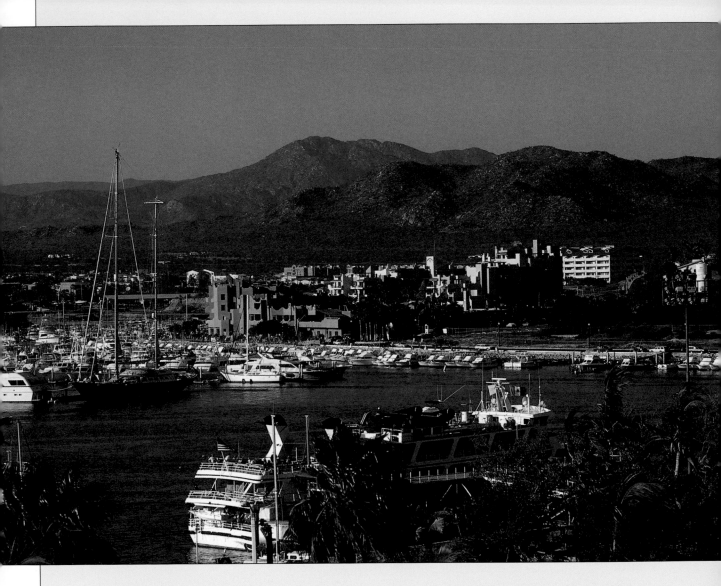

Cabo San Lucas in Baja California Sur is an important port; it receives imported goods, as well as cruise ships full of tourists. Though Mexico's economy is not always stable, it is helped by foreign money through those two avenues.

eruptions are always a threat throughout the Trans-Mexican Volcanic Belt. Mexico is an important part of the Pacific's "Ring of Fire," a circle of active volcanoes.

From the heights of the frozen land to the sands of her hot, dry Chihuahuan Desert, Mexico is a land of extremes. At one moment, it is cool and serene. The next moment, it may be hot and turbulent. Its climate, tropical storms, hurricanes, tsunamis, earthquakes, and volcanic eruptions all join in to create the spicy mixture that is Mexico.

TEXT-DEPENDENT QUESTIONS

At what altitude is the "frozen land" (Tierra Helada) found?
During what months is the threat of hurricanes highest in Mexico?

RESEARCH PROJECT

Using the Internet or your school library, find out about the sort of creatures that live in the deserts of Mexico. Choose one, and write a short report about it. Tell what the animal looks like, whether it is dangerous, what it eats, and how it survives in the harsh climate. Find photos online to include with your report, and present it to the class.

WORDS TO UNDERSTAND

badlands—a region with little plant life.

coral reefs—accumulations beneath the ocean of the skeletal remains of a sea creature, which form hard structures.

hydroelectric—relating to the production of electricity through waterpower.

navigable—able to be traveled by boats.

reservoir—an artificial lake where water is collected and kept for use.

sombrero—a wide-brimmed Mexican hat.

tectonic plates—the large chunks of the earth's crust that sometime shift, creating earthquakes.

View of the Southern Sierra Madre range, which stretches about 620 miles (1,000 km) from southern Michoacán and Guerrero to the Isthmus of Tehuantepec in Oaxaca.

TOPOGRAPHY:
LIKE A SOMBRERO

Like a *sombrero*, all sides of the Mexican mainland slope upward toward the central region. The central region is an elevated plain surrounded by mountains. The Mexican *altiplano*, or central plain, runs between the Eastern and Western Sierra Madre mountain chains. Altiplano means "high plain."

A plain is a broad, flat, or gently rolling area. Plains are usually low in elevation, but most of Mexico's plains are high plains or plateaus. A plateau is flat highland area, often with one steep face. Basically, a plateau is an elevated plain.

High plateaus and mountains cover two thirds of the country. Still, Mexico manages to cling to its diversity. The bright beautiful sombrero that is Mexico's mainland is embroidered with a distinctive patchwork of earth-toned deserts, jewel-painted tropical forests, water-colored coastlines, and grassy green valleys.

Mexico has three major mountain ranges and one volcanic belt. The mountain ranges are all part of the Sierra Madre mountain chain—the Eastern Sierra Madres, or Sierra Madre Orientals; the Western Sierra Madres, or Sierra

29

Madre Occidentals; and the Southern Sierra Madres, or the Sierra Madres del Sur. The Trans-Mexican Volcanic Belt runs from east to west in southern Mexico.

The Western Sierra Madre Range starts beneath the Arizona border. The mountains then run south to the Santiago River. Here they turn into the Trans-Mexican Volcanic Belt. The belt runs east and west. The northwest coastal plain is the lowland area between the Western Sierra Madre and the Gulf of California. The Western Sierra Madre Mountains average 7,425 feet (2,250 meters) in elevation, with peaks reaching almost 10,000 feet (3,000 meters).

The Eastern Sierra Madre Mountains start at the Big Bend region of the Texas-Mexico border. The range runs southward. It, too, meets the Trans-Mexican Volcanic Belt in the South. The northeast coastal plain sprawls from east of the Eastern Sierra Madre to the Gulf of Mexico. The average elevation of the Sierra Madre Oriental is 7,260 feet (2,200 meters), with some peaks at nearly 10,000 feet (3,000 meters).

There is one other major mountain range in the northern half of Mexico. The Sierra de la Giganta runs from the United States border to the southern end of the Baja Peninsula. Its peaks range in altitude from 7,260 feet in the north to only 825 feet (250 meters). This range plunges into the Sea of Cortés near La Paz in the south. Narrow lowlands are found to the east and west of these mountains.

The Trans-Mexican Volcanic Belt is 558 miles (900 kilometers) long and 80 miles (130 kilometers) wide. It stretches from the Pacific Ocean to the Gulf of Mexico. The belt starts at the Río Grande de Santiago. From there, it spreads south to Colima, and from Colima, the belt runs east to the center of the state of Veracruz.

The belt contains Mexico's highest volcanic peaks; three peaks are higher than 1,500 feet (5,000 meters). Pico de Orizaba, found in the belt, is the third

The agave plant is capable of growing in somewhat arid conditions. Its spiny leaves are sometimes cultivated for their fiber or sap.

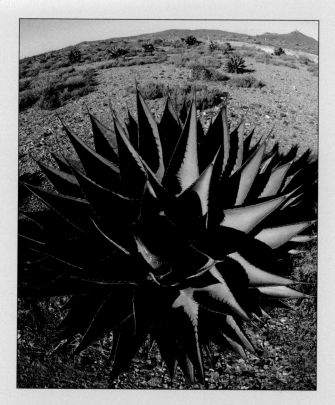

31

highest mountain in North America. Pico de Orizaba is 18,406 feet high (5,610 meters). The belt's other two great peaks are Popocatépetl and Iztaccíhuatl.

Whether from volcanoes or earthquakes, like a jumping bean, Mexico is almost always in motion. This is because Mexico sits right on top of three large *tectonic plates*. These plates are called the American, Caribbean, and the Cocos. The motion of these plates causes earthquakes and volcanic activity. The Baja California Peninsula is on the Pacific Plate. Earthquakes in this region pulled the Baja California Peninsula away from the coast. This created the Gulf of California.

Along Mexico's southern coast ambles the Sierra Madre del Sur. The southern Sierra Madres stretch from the southwestern part of the Trans-Mexican Volcanic Belt to the Isthmus of Tehuantepec. (An isthmus is a piece of land that joins two larger pieces of land together.) Mountains in this range average more than 6,000 feet (2,000 meters) in elevation.

The Río Grande forms part of the boundary between the United States and Mexico. It flows 1,885 miles, from the San Juan Mountains in Colorado to the Gulf of Mexico. This photo shows the river flowing through Big Bend National Park on the Texas-Mexico border.

Pico de Orizaba is the starting point for the Sierra Madre de Oaxaca. This range ends at the Isthmus of Tehuantepec. Summits in the Sierra Madre de Oaxaca average more than 8,000 feet (2,500 meters) in elevation, with some mountains exceeding 10,000 feet.

The Sierra Madre de Chiapas run along the Pacific Coast, south of the Isthmus of Tehuantepec. These mountains stretch from the Oaxaca-Chiapas border to the Mexico-Guatemala border. The average height of the mountains in this range is only 5,000 feet (1,500 meters). Volcán de Tacuma towers above most of the range, reaching over 4,000 meters in height.

Much of Mexico's land may be mountainous, but most of Mexico's population lives on its central plateau. This area of Mexico is in between the Western Sierra Madre and the Eastern Sierra Madre mountain ranges. The plateau generally ranges in elevation from about 3,000 feet (900 meters) in its northern regions to about 8,000 feet (about 2,400 meters) in the south.

Think of Mexico's two peninsulas as the strings that would secure the sombrero around the wearer's neck. The Baja California Peninsula of northwestern Mexico is directly south of California. It contains the states of Baja California Norte and Baja California Sur. The peninsula separates the Gulf of California from the Pacific Ocean. (The Gulf of California is also known as the Sea of Cortés.) The Yucatán Peninsula juts out to the northeast from the Isthmus of Tehuantepec. It extends into the Gulf of Mexico.

The Baja Peninsula is about 760 miles (about 1,200 kilometers) long. It varies in width from 30 to 150 miles (48 to 241 kilometers). Baja California Norte, with its capital city of Mexicali, is in the north. Baja California Sur, with its capital city of La Paz, is in the south.

The Baja California Peninsula has three main mountain ranges. The Sierra de la Giganta run along the eastern coast of the state of Baja California Sur, with peaks more than 10,000 feet (3,000 meters) above sea level. The Sierra de San Borja are found in the southern region of Baja California Norte. The Sierra de San Pedro Mártir are found in the northern region of Baja California Norte.

The Yucatán Peninsula is made up of flat lowlands. The northwestern peninsula is dry and brushy, while in the south, where rainfall is abundant, the peninsula is covered by tropical rain forests.

The narrowest part of Mexico, between the gulfs of Campeche and Tehuantepec, is the Isthmus of Tehuantepec. This isthmus is approximately 130 miles wide at its narrowest point. The Isthmus of Tehuantepec is all that separates the Gulf of Mexico from the Pacific Ocean along this section of Mexico.

The Isthmus of Tehuantepec is a gently sloped lowland region. The northern side of the isthmus is wet, swampy, and thickly covered with jungle. Its southern Pacific slopes are drier. The lowest point of the isthmus is at about 754 feet (230 meters) above sea level.

Mexico has almost 150 rivers. Most of these rivers drain into the Pacific Ocean. Few of them flow into the Gulf of Mexico or the Caribbean Sea. Water is a precious commodity in many areas, because of the locations of the major rivers.

Mexico has five major rivers. All five of these rivers flow into the Gulf of Mexico. Northern and central Mexico, home to almost 60 percent of Mexico's population, have less than 10 percent of the country's water resources.

The Grijalva River begins in Guatemala, then flows through the state of Chiapas, and empties into the Gulf of Mexico near Villahermosa. It is one of Mexico's few rivers that are **navigable**, but small boats can travel on only a few areas of the river.

The Usumacinta River also starts in Guatemala. It travels east through Chiapas, and then meets and joins the Grijalva River near the Gulf of Mexico.

The Infiernillo Dam is on the Balsas River southwest of Mexico City. This dam helps to contain one of the largest water **reservoirs** in the country. It runs along the border between the states of Guerrero and Michoacán.

The Papaloapan River originates in the mountains north of the Isthmus of Tehuantepec and then flows east. The Papaloapan River empties into the Gulf of Mexico near Coatzacoalcos.

Two rivers form the largest and most important river system in Mexico. The Grande de Santiago and Lerma Rivers flow into and out of Lake Chapala. The Lerma begins in the Western Sierra Madre and flows into Lake Chapala, while the Grande de Santiago flows out of the Lake Chapala and empties into the

Pacific Ocean. The Grande de Santiago serves as a major source of *hydroelectric* power.

The Río Grande winds along the entire Texas-Mexico border. Farmers in both the United States and the United Mexican States have come to depend upon the Río Grande. It is a major source of water for irrigation projects in both Texas and Mexico.

Lakes and lagoons are very important in Mexico. Lakes are inland bodies of water that do not touch the sea. Lagoons are found along the coasts, and are separated from the sea by only a strip of land. Like Mexico's rivers, their water is used for agriculture irrigation projects. Without them, Mexico's farmers would have very little farming success. Mexico does not have a large number of lagoons and lakes, however. The largest lakes in the Republic of Mexico are Lakes Chapala, Cuitzeo, and Pátzcuaro. The largest lagoons are the lagoons of Tamiahua and Términos.

Lake Chapala is south of the city of Guadalajara. It is the largest lake in the country, about 50 miles (80 kilometers) long and about 8 miles (13 kilometers) at its widest point. Lake Xochimilco is south of Mexico City in the Valley of Mexico. It is one of the most famous lakes in all of Mexico.

Mexico has three major gulfs. A gulf is part of a sea or ocean that reaches into the land. It is usually larger than a bay. The Gulf of Mexico is found on the eastern coast of Mexico. The Gulf of California, or the Sea of Cortez, is between the Baja Peninsula and the western coast of mainland Mexico. The Gulf of Tehuantepec is located along the southwestern Mexico along the western coast of the Isthmus of Tehuantepec.

Mexico has many bays along its coastlines. A bay is also a part of a body of salt water that reaches inland, but it is generally smaller in size than a gulf.

36

The Bay of Sebastián Vizcaíno lies along the west of the Baja California Peninsula. The Island of Cedros is located between it and the Pacific Ocean. Within the Gulf of California, along the eastern coast of the Baja Peninsula, are the Bay of Coyote, the Bay of Los Angeles, and the Bay of Santa Ana. Along the western coast of mainland Mexico, within the Gulf of California, are the Bay of Adair, the Bay of Tepoca, and the Bay of Santa Maria.

The Yucatán Peninsula has several bays along the Caribbean Sea. The bays of Calderitas, Espíritu Santo, and the Ascension extend inland from the Caribbean to the Yucatán Peninsula. Along the Yucatán's Gulf of Mexico coastline are a number of lagoons.

Mexico's coastline is one of the longest in the world. It is about 5,800 miles long (9,330 kilometers). Mexico's western coast is almost twice the length of its eastern coast.

Veracruz, Tampico, and Coatzacoalcos are the major eastern ports. They are all on the Gulf of Mexico. Acapulco, Manzanillo, Mazatlán, and Salina Cruz are the major ports in the west. These ports are along the North Pacific Ocean.

Mexico's many islands are as diverse as the different regions of its mainland. Two important islands in the Gulf of California are Ángel de la Guarda (Island of the Guardian Angel) and Tiburón (Shark Island). Cozumel and the Island of Women are two important islands in

Lake Xochimilco is known for its floating gardens. The lake is just south of Mexico City. The Aztecs piled layers of mud and marsh plants into the lake to create small islands. They then planted flowers and plants on these little islands (known as chinampas). The islands do not really float, although they look as if they do. The chinampas of Lake Xochimilco still provide the citizens of Mexico City with fresh flowers and vegetables to this day.

Fishing boats are anchored near the statue of "Jesus the Fisherman" in Lake Chapala, Jalisco. Fishing is an important source of revenue and food for Mexican families living along the coast and near large bodies of water.

A diver interacts with a Hawksbill Turtle at the coral reef near Cozumel.

the Gulf of Mexico. The Island of Guadalupe is in the Pacific Ocean.

The Island of Guadalupe is Mexico's westernmost island off Baja California. It is approximately 160 miles (258 kilometers) from shore. This is a volcanic oceanic island. It is about 22 miles (35 kilometers) long and about 4 to 6 miles (7 to 10 kilometers) wide. There is very little fresh water on the island, and it is particularly scarce at the higher altitudes of the island. The island reaches elevations of 4,200 feet (1,280 meters) at its northern end.

Cozumel is Mexico's largest inhabited island. The island is located just 12 miles (19 kilometers) off the Yucatán Coast. It is 29 miles (47 kilometers) long and 10 miles (15 kilometers) wide. Cozumel is actually divided into a coastal city and an island city.

A dense jungle covers Cozumel's interior, while its beaches are covered with ivory white sands. Cozumel's shore is home to one of the most dramatic collections of **coral reefs** in the Gulf of Mexico.

The Isla Mujeres, or the Island of Women, is located just eight miles across the Bahía de Mujeres (Bay of Women) from Cancún. The Island of Women is only 5 miles (8 kilometers) long and half a mile wide. The average temperature is 80° Fahrenheit (27° Celsius). The island's terrain is flat, with beaches on all sides.

The Island of the Guardian Angel and Shark Island divide the Gulf of California into two sections. Shark Island is an island off the coast of Sonora. It is the largest island in all of Mexico, approximately 31 miles (50 kilometers) long and 15.5 miles (25 kilometers) wide), with a surface area of about 480 square miles (1,208 square kilometers). It is home to two low mountain ranges that reach heights of up to 400 feet (1,315 meters) above sea level.

The Island of the Guardian Angel is the second largest island in the Gulf of California. It is 43 miles (70 kilometers) long and about 12 miles (20 kilometers) at its widest, and its surface area is roughly 533 square miles (about 895 square kilometers). It is made up of a steep mountain range so that the island literally rises from the seabed. The mountains of Guardian Angel

The second-largest coral reef in the world starts at Cozumel. It is the exotic black coral reef called Palancar Reef. Jacques Costeau is credited with discovering it.

Wildflowers grow in the Sonoran Desert. In the background are the Sierra Pinacate, a group of volcanic mountains located in the state of Sonora that rise to a height of 3,904 ft (1,190 m).

Island reach a maximum height of about 1,315 feet (400 meters) at the north end of the island.

In the northwest of Mexico, including much of the Baja Peninsula, lies the Sonoran Desert. This desert is as diverse as the rest of Mexico. In places, it is perhaps the most fertile *badland* of them all. In others, it is the harshest desert climate in North America.

The Grand Desert region of the Sonoran Desert is located in Mexico to the east of the Colorado River. It is home to the harshest, sandiest, most wind-blown desert terrain. The region of the Sonoran Desert that is found

Cozumel is warm all year long, with an average temperature of 81°F (27°C). Heavy rains start in June and go on through October.

41

within the state of Sonora has a longer, wetter summer rainy season with a drier winter. The Sonoran Desert on Baja is often called the Vizcaíno Desert.

The Chihuahuan Desert is the easternmost and southernmost of the four North American deserts: the Great Basin Desert, the Sonoran Desert, the Mojave Desert, and the Chihuahuan Desert. Much of the Chihuahuan Desert lies within the boundaries of the Mexican Plateau. It is bounded on the west by the Sierra Madre Occidental and on the east by the Sierra Madre Oriental, with its southern boundary in Zacatecas. It extends from Mexico into southeastern Arizona, southern New Mexico, and Trans-Pecos Texas.

TEXT-DEPENDENT QUESTIONS

What is the largest lake in Mexico? Where is it located?

What is Mexico's largest inhabited island?

RESEARCH PROJECT

Make a topographic map of Mexico. First, trace the country's outline onto a large piece of cardboard. Next, do some research to find out where various natural features, such as mountains and rivers are located. Using modeling clay, create mountains and plateaus, and glue them onto the cardboard in the area where they are located. Use paint to color your model and add in rivers and other natural features.

WORDS TO UNDERSTAND

cacao—the bean used to make chocolate.

chicle—sap from the sapodilla tree that is used to make chewing gum.

Mardi Gras—a carnival celebration on the Tuesday before the beginning of Lent, the six weeks of fasting before Easter.

serapes—colorful woolen shawls worn by Mexican women.

sinkholes—hollow places where water collects; often connect with an underground cavern or passage.

Mexico's dense tropical jungles are home to thousands of rare plant, animal and insect species.

THE REGIONS OF MEXICO

The majority of Mexicans live, work, and play on the Mexican Plateau. The plateau can be divided into two major parts: the Northern Plateau and the Central Plateau.

The Northern Region of the Central Plateau begins near the U.S. border. It ends near San Luis Potosí. In this dryer part of the Mexican Plateau, few people live. Those who do, live around the areas that lend themselves to irrigation.

In the Salado River valley of the Northern Plateau, wheat is grown. In its Laguna Basin area, much of Mexico's cotton is grown. Other crops include corn (maize), beans, and alfalfa, and large areas of the more arid land are utilized as rangeland for cattle. There are few permanent streams in this region.

The Central Plateau is often called the "Mexican Heartland." This is because the Central Plateau has some of Mexico's most fertile farmland. The temperate climate combined with the fairly abundant rainfall and rich volcanic soils make this region very good for farming.

The Central Plateau is used for raising cattle in some of its drier areas to the north. The major crops raised in this region are corn, beans, wheat, and sugarcane. There are sugar refineries and grain mills in Guadalajara.

The Central Plateau is home to many important Mexican industries, such as

44

textiles, cement, and chemicals. The major cities within the Central Plateau are Mexico City, Guadalajara, León, Querétaro, and Pachuca. These cities have flourished for many years around the fertile farmlands and industry-friendly landscape of the Central Plateau.

The states of Coahuila, Chihuahua, and Nuevo León make up the mountainous northern region of Mexico. Coahuila's capital is Saltillo. It is about 530 feet (1,748 meters) above sea level. This state is famous for its brightly colored handwoven *serapes*.

Monterrey, the capital city of Nuevo León, is famous for being the third largest city in Mexico, as well as a major center of industry. Twenty-five percent of Mexico's manufactured goods are made in and around this city.

Chihuahua City is the capital of Mexico's largest state. Birthplace of the Chihuahua dog, this state is also home to Mexico's large sect of Mennonites. Chihuahua is the state where Mexico's Copper Canyon and the Basaseachi Falls can be found.

The Baja California Peninsula starts in the far northwest of the country. It stretches southeast 800 miles (1,290 kilometers) from its U.S. border. The Baja California Peninsula is dry and mountainous, while its coastal plain is very narrow. U.S. tourists visit coastal

Chihuahua is home to the Tarahumara Indians. An estimated 50,000 Tarahumara still live in small shacks and caves deep within the Sierra Madres and the Copper Canyon. The Tarahumara live as traditionally as possible, shunning the modern technology that most Mexicans have come to take for granted. Their main diet consists of corn tortillas, potatoes, beans, and squash. Their religion is a mix of traditional Indian practices and those brought to them by the Catholic missionaries. The Tarahumara worship the sun and the moon, as well as Jesus Christ, the Christian God, and the Catholic saints.

Cañón del Sumidero cuts through the Mexican state of Chiapas. Mexico's varied landscape features countless natural land formations.

45

resorts along the northern Gulf of California and on the Pacific Ocean. The rest of the peninsula is only sparsely inhabited. The Baja Peninsula is home to the states of Baja California Norte and Baja California Sur.

The Gulf Coast plain lies between the Eastern Sierra Madre and the Gulf of Mexico. The coast is made up mainly of swampland and lagoons. Its northern region is dry. In the south, are tropical forests. The southern part of the Gulf Coast Plain, where there is much more rain, is home to some fertile farming lands.

Veracruz, Mexico's most important port, is located in this region. Many of Mexico's oil finds have taken place in this area. Veracruz is also a favorite vacation destination for many Mexicans. As a result, the people of Veracruz are chiefly employed by the tourist and oil industries. They are known throughout Mexico for their love of *Mardi Gras* and music. Veracruz is said to be the home of the music called "La Bamba." Veracruz is also known to

46

Fertile pasturelands stretch across the mountains of Mexico. Agriculture remains an important industry in Mexico, where it keeps the demand for imported goods at a reasonable level.

celebrate Mardi Gras with a zest that is rivaled only by that of New Orleans.

The Pacific Lowlands lie between the Western Sierra Madre and the Pacific Ocean. The northern regions are irrigated and used for farming. To the south of Manzanillo, they are bordered by the Sierra Madre del Sur. Mazatlán, Puerto Vallarta, and Manzanillo are three of the important cities found along the Pacific lowland coast.

Many of the people in and around the city of Mazatlán are fishermen, farmers, artisans, and tourist service workers. Mazatlán is also home to Mexico's largest shrimp fleet. The surrounding area farms produce melons, tomatoes, cantaloupes, wheat, and cotton.

The artisans of Concordia, a town 30 miles (48 kilometers) southeast of Mazatlán, produce furniture and pottery. Concordia is proud of its furniture-making tradition. The city center is decorated with an oversized rocking chair in honor of the town's furniture makers.

Oaxaca, Chiapas, and Tabasco are the major Mexican states of the tropical south. The rugged southern state of Oaxaca is only 150 miles (242 kilometers) distant from Mexico City. With the mountains as a barrier to the capital city, however, Oaxaca seems like an entire world away from modern Mexico City. Life is lived more leisurely in Oaxaca than it is in Mexico City, and the population is much smaller. The citizens of Oaxaca are artists, farmers, and weavers. There is no commercial industry or big business here. Although the landscape is rocky and dry, Oaxaca is home to a large Indian population. These Indians are said to produce the finest handicrafts in all of Mexico.

Oaxaca the city is a popular destination for tourists. Thriving village markets surround the city. It is also close to some of Mexico's most spectacular pre-Hispanic Indian ruins. Monte Albán and Yagul are both found within the borders of Oaxaca's Central Valley.

Tabasco is a region of equatorial rainforests. Many rivers run through the state on their way to the Gulf of Mexico. Petroleum and other mineral deposits have led to a chemical industrial boom here. It is a very wealthy state, but Tabasco, homeland of the ancient Olmecs, tends to be sparsely populated. The only heavily populated area is the city of Villahermosa. On the banks of the Grijalva River, this boomtown is famous for its extreme tropical heat and humidity. The ruins of the ancient Olmecs' Comalcalco are close to this city.

Directly south of Tabasco is the poorer state of Chiapas. Although this state faces serious economic struggles, it is nevertheless rich with tremendous diversity. For instance, Chiapas is covered with many volcanic mountains. At the center of Chiapas is San Cristóbal de Las Casas, a colonial town seated in the midst of a collection of traditional Indian villages. To the north, the Chiapan rainforest wraps itself around many Mayan ruins. The Agua Azul waterfalls of

47

this region rank among Mexico's most spectacular sights, and the El Triunfo cloud forest in Chiapas dwells beneath an almost constant cloud cover. Combine almost constant rainfall with the cloud cover, and this becomes one of Mexico's wettest and greenest areas. The cloud forest is an ideal habitat for Mexico's quetzal bird, a bird with green tail feathers that reach up to two feet long.

The Yucatán Peninsula is a flat, low-lying region. It reaches northeast from the Isthmus of Tehuantepec into the Gulf of Mexico. Natural **sinkholes** that speckle the landscape of the northern Yucatán were once its only source of water. The important international tourist center of Cancún is located along the eastern coast of the Yucatán.

The northwestern region of the Yucatán Peninsula is dry and brushy. It supports very little farming. In the south, however, rainfall is plentiful. The southern Yucatán Peninsula is covered with tropical rain forests.

The three states that make up the Yucatán Peninsula are Campeche, Yucatán, and Quintana Roo. The people of this

Tarahumara Indian women gather in a town plaza in Mexico. The women wear serapes, which are often brilliantly colored wraps.

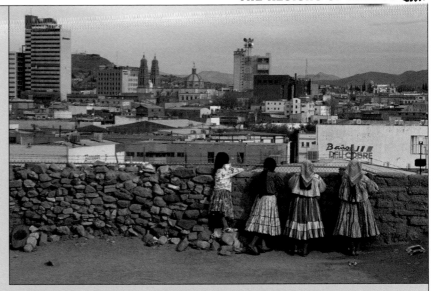

Four young Mexican girls watch the skyline in Chihuahua City. Although Mexico's economy has been gradually improving over the years, the cities are home to many impoverished families.

region are called Yucatecos. Many Yucatecos are descendants of the Mayan Indians who lived in Yucatán hundreds of years before the Spaniards arrived. A great majority of the Yucatecos are farmers.

Northern Yucatán is an important henequén farming region. Henequén is used to make twine and rope. Other crops grown on the Yucatán Peninsula include *cacao*, *chicle*, coffee, corn, cotton, sugar cane, and tobacco. Cacao is used to make chocolate. Chicle is used to make chewing gum.

TEXT-DEPENDENT QUESTIONS
What Mexican states are located on the Baja Peninsula?
Where are the Pacific Lowlands of Mexico located?

RESEARCH PROJECT
Cañón del Sumidero began to be formed at around the same time as the Grand Canyon in the United States. Using the Internet or your school library, find out more about these two amazing natural wonders. In what ways are the similar? How are they different? Compile the information and share it with your class.

WORDS TO UNDERSTAND

cenote—a natural pit or sinkhole that occurs when limestone bedrock collapses, exposing groundwater underneath.

sanctuary—an area in which certain types of wildlife, flora, or fauna are protected, for the purpose of conservation as well as to provide opportunities for scientific study.

The Popocatépetl volcano lets out a plume of smoke in Puebla, Mexico. This active volcano has erupted many times over the past two decades, most recently in 2012 and 2013.

NATIONAL PARKS AND NATURAL WONDERS

Mexico has nearly 60 national parks and biosphere reserves. As the nation's interest in conservation grows, so does its number of parks and reserves. The country is also home to many natural wonders that have not as of yet been declared national parks or reserves.

Popocatépetl and Iztaccihuatl National Park is just outside Mexico City. It is home to the two well-known and well-loved volcanoes, Popo and Izta. Visitors used to climb Popocatépetl. In recent decades, however, the volcano's rumblings have been too strong for government officials to allow mountain climbing. Izta is still open for climbing. It stands about 19,000 feet (5,780 meters) in the air. Izta is a challenge to even experienced mountain climbers.

For those visitors to Mexico who would rather swim than climb, the Sea of Cortés is a favorite vacation destination. Mexico's Sea of Cortés has been declared a whale **sanctuary**, because the waters are the breeding and birthing grounds for gray whales. The whales travel from the Arctic waters of Alaska's Bering Sea to the warm waters off the coast of Baja California. The whales arrive at the Sea of Cortés between December and January, and they stay at least until March but sometimes as late as June.

Mexico has interesting bodies of water *beneath* its ground, as well as along its shores. The **cenotes**, or wells, of the Yucatán are caverns that house underground rivers. These are natural wells, which at one time supplied water to ancient people. The Mayans treated some cenotes as sacred places. They would come to them to hold religious rites and to make sacrifices.

The beaches of the Yucatán are the nesting grounds for several different species of sea turtles. The loggerhead turtle is one of these species. Kemp's Ridley turtles, another species, follow two major migration routes in the Gulf of Mexico: one northward to the Mississippi area, the other southward to the Campeche Bank, near the Yucatán Peninsula. The green sea turtle is also found in this region.

 Mexican folklore refers to Popocatépetl as a great Aztec warrior who was disappointed in love. According to folklore, Popocatépetl and the nearby dormant Iztaccíhuatl volcanoes were once star-crossed Aztec lovers. A rumor spread, saying that the warrior had been killed in battle. Hearing these rumors, Iztaccíhuatl's father forced her to marry another man. She killed herself in despair. Popocatépetl returned home from battle to find his beloved Iztaccíhuatl dead. Overcome with grief, the warrior lifted the woman's dead body and carried her off to the forest where he lay her down gently. The saddened warrior then waited patiently for his love to awaken and come back to him. He is still waiting. This is supposedly why the volcano smokes and rumbles so often. It is the spirit of Popocatépetl bemoaning the death of his love.

"Popocatépetl" means "Smoking Mountain" in the indigenous Nahuatl language. The residents of Mexico refer to the volcano simply, as "Popo." Popocatépetl is thought to be over 10,000 years old. Hernán Cortés wrote about seeing this volcano erupt in 1519.

53

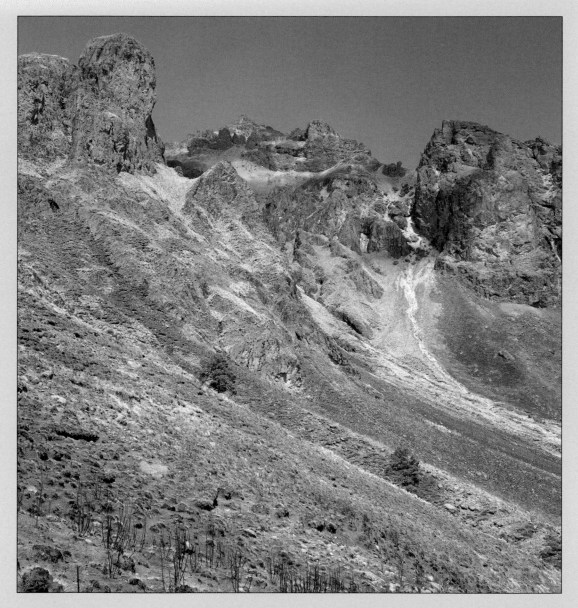

Popocatépetl's sister volcano, Ixtaccihuatl. The volcanoes and the land surrounding them have been designated a national park by the Mexican government.

54

The Acapulco beach in Guerrero is one of Mexico's popular resort locations. Mexico's clean white sand beaches are considered some of the most beautiful in the world.

Every fall, millions of Monarch butterflies begin their annual journey to Michoacán, Mexico. This is one of nature's greatest natural phenomena. The orange and black butterflies travel distances of up to 3,100 miles (5,000 kilometers) to avoid the north's winter freezes. From Canada and the United States, the Monarch begins its month-long trip in late October or early November. The butterflies travel more than 70 miles (approximately 112 kilometers) per day. Fortunate viewers can see large groups of butterflies flying overhead. The butterflies fly steadily toward central Mexico's mountaintop pine forests. Their journey ends in the eastern mountains surrounding Morelia, Michoacán's capital. Here in the Oyamel fir forests, the Monarch spends its winter waiting for spring. When springtime finally comes, the butterflies mate. Afterward, they return north. They lay their eggs along their way home.

Located in the Lacandona Rainforest, along the Guatemalan border, is the national park of the Montebello Lakes. There are 59 lakes in this park, including a group of five known as Lakes of Colors. These lakes vary in color from steel gray and emerald green to amethyst and turquoise. The colors are created by mineral deposits.

Mexico's butterfly-filled forests, beaches covered with nesting sea turtles, mineral-colored lakes, smoldering volcanoes, whale birthing grounds, and once-sacred underground wells all combine to create a rainbow of national parks and natural wonders. Like a kaleidoscope, Mexico's national parks and natural wonders are constantly

The Copper Canyon is in northern Mexico within the state of Chihuahua. It is four times bigger than Arizona's Grand Canyon. The Copper Canyon is almost 300 feet (about 100 meters) deeper than the Grand Canyon.

The Copper Canyon area of Mexico is made up of over 900 miles (1,450 kilometers) of canyons. The canyon system is so large and so deep, that it has mountains within canyons. There are five major canyons in this area.

The Urique River, once a powerful, rushing torrent, carved the main part of the canyon. Today, the Urique River is a small, mild-mannered stream.

Although the trains of the Copper Canyon Railroad also haul timber, it caters mainly to tourists who wish to view this great natural wonder. The Copper Canyon Railroad carries its riders over awe-inspiring chasms, through traditional Tarahumara Indian villages, past rushing rivers, and along alpine forests. The ride from Chihuahua to Los Mochis takes approximately 12 hours. There are 87 tunnels and 35 bridges along the way.

The annual migration of Monarch butterflies is one of Mexico's unique natural attractions, drawing tourists and nature lovers to Michoacán. The butterflies spend several months in the Mexican forest before returning north. Unfortunately, in recent years the Monarch butterfly population has declined drastically, and scientists are not certain why. In 1996, the Mexican butterfly population was estimated at 1 billion; by January 2014, the Monarch population had fallen to just 33 million.

The blue-green waters of Lake Esmeralda, one of the five lakes known in Mexico as the Lagunas de Colores (Lakes of Colors). The others are Encantada, Ensueño, Agua Tinta, and Bosque Azul.)

changing. They are also, like Mexico, unique and diverse. Mexico's geography is, indeed, an ever-changing kaleidoscope of beauty and diversity.

TEXT-DEPENDENT QUESTIONS

What is a cenote? What were these used for by the ancient people of Mexico?

RESEARCH PROJECT

If you'd like to help contribute to the Monarch butterfly population, plant milkweed in or near your garden. In late spring, start looking on the underside of leaves for small white dots—these are monarch eggs. You can bring the leaves with eggs inside, and put them into a large container with a lid (make sure there are air holes in the top). Once they hatch, the caterpillars will eat the leaves; you'll have to add fresh milkweed leaves daily. The caterpillar stage will last for a couple of weeks, then they will hang from a branch in their container, or even from the lid, form a cocoon. Place the container in an area where it won't be shaken and keep an eye on the cocoons. They will turn darker once they are nearly ready to hatch, which occurs in early September. Release them immediately once they hatch into butterflies, so they can begin their journey to Mexico.

SERIES GLOSSARY

Adobe	A building material made of mud and straw.
Amerindian	A term for the indigenous peoples of North and South America before the arrival of Europeans in the late 15th century.
Conquistador	Any one of the Spanish leaders of the conquest of the Americas in the 1500s.
Criollo	A resident of New Spain who was born in North America to parents of Spanish ancestry. In the social order of New Spain, criollos ranked above mestizos.
Fiesta	A Mexican party or celebration.
Haciendas	Large Mexican ranches.
Maquiladoras	Factories created to attract foreign business to Mexico by allowing them to do business cheaply.
Mariachi	A Mexican street band that performs a distinctive type of music utilizing guitars, violins, and trumpets.
Mesoamerica	The region of southern North America that was inhabited before the arrival of the Spaniards.
Mestizo	A person of mixed Amerindian and European (typically Spanish) descent.
Nahuatl	The ancient language spoken by the Aztecs; still spoken by many modern Mexicans.
New Spain	Name for the Spanish colony that included modern-day Mexico. This vast area of North America was conquered by Spain in the 1500s and ruled by the Spanish until 1821.
Plazas	The central open squares at the center of Spanish cities.
Pre-Columbian	Referring to a time before the 1490s, when Christopher Columbus landed in the Americas.

58

FURTHER READING

Berdan, Frances F. *Aztec Archaeology and Ethnohistory*. London: Cambridge University Press, 2014.

Burton, Tony, and Richard Rhoda. *Geo-Mexico: the Geography and Dynamics of Modern Mexico*. Ladysmith, British Columbia, Canada: Sombrero Books, 2010.

Craib, Raymond B. *Cartographic Mexico*. Durham, N.C.: Duke University Press, 2004.

Foster, Lynn V. *A Brief History of Mexico*. New York: Checkmark Books, 2007.

Franz, Carl, et al. *The People's Guide to Mexico*. Berkeley, Calif.: Avalon Travel Publishing, 2006.

Golden, Nancy. *Exploring Mexico With the Five Themes of Geography*. New York: Rosen, 2005.

Gritzner, Charles F. *Mexico*. New York: Chelsea House, 2012.

Kent, Deborah. *Mexico*. New York: Children's Press, 2012.

Mayor, Guy. *Mexico: A Quick Guide to Customs and Etiquette*. New York: Kuperard, 2006.

Muller, Peter O., and Elizabeth Muller-Hames. *Geography Study Guide: Realms, Regions, and Concepts*. Hoboken, N.J.: John Wiley and Sons, 2005.

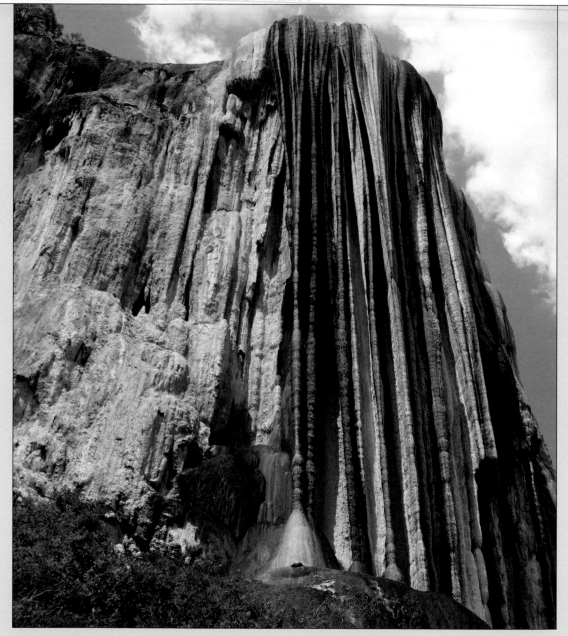

View from below Hierve el Agua, an unusual rock formation in Oaxaca in which mineral deposits have formed stalactite-like shapes that resemble a waterfall.

INTERNET RESOURCES

Facts and figures about Mexico's geography
http://www.mexonline.com/geography.htm

Mesoweb
http://www.mesoweb.com/welcome.html#externalresources

National Geographic
http://kids.nationalgeographic.com/kids/places/find/mexico
http://travel.nationalgeographic.com/travel/countries/mexico-guide

CIA World Factbook
https://www.cia.gov/library/publications/the-world-factbook/geos/mx.html

History of Mexico
http://www.history.com/topics/mexico

Information about Mexico and its Geography
http://www.infoplease.com/country/mexico.html

INDEX

63

PICTURE CREDITS

ABOUT THE AUTHOR

Colleen Madonna Flood Williams holds a bachelor's degree in elementary education, with a minor in art. She is the author of numerous study units, magazine articles, newspaper articles, essays, and poems. Colleen lives in Soldotna, Alaska, with her husband Paul, her son Dillon, and their Bouvier des Flandres dog, Kosmos Kramer.